the
super bowl
50 Delicious Dips

Printed in the United States of America
by G&R Publishing Co.

Distributed By:

507 Industrial Street
Waverly, IA 50677

ISBN-13: 978-1-56383-292-5
ISBN-10: 1-56383-292-5
Item # 3612

Table of Contents

Chunky Tomato Dip

Makes 2 to 3 cups

Ingredients

3 cloves garlic, minced

2 T. olive oil

2 (14.5 oz.) cans diced
tomatoes, drained

¼ C. tomato paste

½ tsp. dried basil

¼ tsp. dried oregano

Directions

In a large saucepan over medium heat, sauté garlic in olive oil until golden. Add diced tomatoes, tomato paste, dried basil and dried oregano. Simmer, uncovered, for 15 to 20 minutes or until sauce is thick enough for dipping. Chill in the refrigerator for 2 hours before serving. Serve with red and green bell pepper strips, celery sticks, soft warm breadsticks, breaded mozzarella sticks and pepperoni slices for dipping.

Bacon Bite Ranch Dip

Makes 3 cups

Ingredients

1 (2.8 oz.) jar bacon pieces
2 C. ranch-style salad dressing
1 C. sour cream

½ C. grated Parmesan cheese
2 green onions, sliced

Directions

In a large bowl, combine bacon pieces, ranch-style dressing, sour cream, grated Parmesan cheese and sliced green onions; mix well. Cover and place in the refrigerator until chilled. Serve with fresh carrot sticks, celery sticks, red and green bell pepper strips, broccoli florets, blanched asparagus, blanched green beans, an assortment of breaded vegetables, crackers and pita chips for dipping.

Dip Tip

Let dips rest before serving. Sometimes dips get even tastier after the ingredients have time to combine. However, make sure the dips stay fresh by keeping warm dips warm and cold dips cold.

Cheesy Corn Dip

Makes 4 to 5 cups

Ingredients

1 (16 oz.) pkg. shredded
  Monterey Jack cheese

2 (4 oz.) cans sliced black
  olives, drained

1 (14.5 oz.) can diced
  tomatoes, drained

4 (4.5 oz.) cans diced green
  chiles, drained

1 bunch green onions, chopped

1 (10 oz.) can white
  corn, drained

1 (16 oz.) bottle Italian
  salad dressing

Directions

In large bowl, combine the shredded Monterey Jack cheese, sliced black olives, diced tomatoes, diced green chiles, chopped green onions and white corn. Pour in Italian salad dressing and stir to coat. Chill in the refrigerator until serving. Serve with tortilla chips, crackers or pita chips for dipping.

Roasted Red Pepper Hummus

Makes 2 cups

Ingredients

2 cloves garlic, minced

1 (15 oz.) can garbanzo beans, drained

⅓ C. tahini

⅓ C. lemon juice

½ C. roasted red peppers

¼ tsp. dried basil

Salt and pepper to taste

Directions

Using a food processor, combine minced garlic, garbanzo beans, tahini and lemon juice; process until smooth. Add the roasted red peppers and basil; process until peppers are finely chopped and season with salt and pepper. Transfer hummus to a small bowl, cover and chill in the refrigerator until serving. Serve with fresh carrot sticks, red and green bell pepper strips, celery sticks, mini pita pockets, pita chips or crackers for dipping.

Dip Tip

Tahini, or sesame paste, is a common ingredient of hummus and other Middle Eastern and East Asian foods. It is sold fresh or dehydrated. Peanut butter can be used as a substitute for tahini, or the ingredient can be omitted.

Tahini-Free Hummus

Makes 2 cups

Ingredients

1 (15 oz.) can garbanzo beans, drained, liquid reserved

1 clove garlic, crushed

2 tsp. ground cumin

½ tsp. salt

1 T. olive oil

Directions

In a blender or food processor, combine garbanzo beans, crushed garlic, ground cumin, salt and olive oil; blend or process on low speed. Add reserved bean liquid gradually; continue to process until desired consistency is reached. Serve with fresh carrot sticks, red and green bell pepper strips, celery sticks, mini pita pockets, pita chips or crackers for dipping.

Garlic Sun-Dried Tomato Dip

Makes 2½ cups

Ingredients

¼ C. oil-packed sun-dried
    tomatoes, drained
    and chopped

1 (8 oz.) pkg. cream cheese,
    softened

½ C. sour cream

¼ C. mayonnaise

2 cloves garlic, minced

Hot pepper sauce to taste

¾ tsp. salt

¾ tsp. pepper

¼ C. fresh basil

Directions

In a food processor, combine the sun-dried tomatoes, cream cheese, sour cream, mayonnaise, minced garlic, hot pepper sauce, salt and pepper; process until smooth. Add basil and process until well combined. Chill in the refrigerator for 1 hour before serving. Serve with fresh carrot sticks, celery sticks, red and green bell pepper strips, baked potato wedges, pita chips or crackers for dipping.

Olive Feta Cheese Dip

Makes 1 ½ cups

Ingredients

1 (6 oz.) pkg. feta
   cheese, crumbled

2 T. olive oil

1 tsp. lemon juice

½ tsp. minced garlic

2 oz. sun-dried
   tomatoes, softened

½ tsp. dried oregano

1 T. chopped black
   olives, drained

Directions

In a food processor, combine feta cheese, olive oil, lemon juice, minced garlic, sun-dried tomatoes and oregano; process until smooth. Transfer the mixture to a medium bowl. Stir in the chopped black olives. Chill in the refrigerator until serving. Serve with crackers, an assortment of breaded vegetables, pita chips or toasted baguette slices for dipping and spreading.

Dip Tip

If a dip thickens too much while chilling in the refrigerator, thin it by stirring in a splash of milk, broth, water or olive oil. It's best to use an ingredient that was included in the recipe. Thinning the dip will make it easier to scoop.

Cocktail Surprise Layer Dip

Makes 4 cups

Ingredients

1 (8 oz.) pkg. cream
cheese, softened

3 T. milk

1 C. cocktail sauce

1 avocado, peeled, pitted
and diced

1 tomato, chopped

1 green bell pepper, chopped

1 bunch green onions, chopped

1 (2 oz.) can black olives,
drained and chopped

1 (8 oz.) pkg. shredded
Cheddar cheese

Directions

In a small bowl, combine the cream cheese and milk; mix until smooth. Spread cream cheese mixture onto a large round serving plate. Spread the cocktail sauce over the cream cheese and top with diced avocado. Layer the chopped tomato, chopped green bell pepper, chopped green onions and chopped black olives over the avocado. Sprinkle with shredded Cheddar cheese. Chill in the refrigerator for 1 hour or until firm. Serve with tortilla chips, crackers or pita chips for dipping and spreading.

Crabmeat Dip

Makes 3½ cups

Ingredients

1½ C. sour cream
1 C. mayonnaise

1 (1.4 oz.) env. dry
   vegetable soup mix
1 C. diced imitation crabmeat

Directions

In a medium bowl, combine sour cream, mayonnaise, vegetable soup mix and imitation crabmeat; mix well. Cover and chill in the refrigerator overnight. Serve with crackers, toasted bread points, potato chips or pita chips for dipping.

Dip Tip

To keep cold dips cold, place your dip bowl in a slightly larger serving bowl. Then, fill the larger bowl with ice to surround the dip bowl.

Simple Shrimp Dip

Makes 2 cups

Ingredients

1 (8 oz.) pkg. cream
cheese, softened

1 C. mayonnaise

¼ C. chopped onion

¼ C. chopped celery

½ lb. cooked, peeled, chopped
and deveined shrimp

Directions

In a medium bowl, combine cream cheese and mayonnaise; mix well. Add the chopped onion, chopped celery and shrimp meat. Cover and chill in the refrigerator until serving. Serve with crackers or pita chips for dipping.

Dip Tip

Although some dips are more flavorful after they've had time to rest and combine, you might need to reseason other dips before serving. Make sure to taste test your dips before you present them to guests. If needed, add a little salt, pepper or splash of lime juice to perk it up!

Ham and Cream Cheese Spread

Makes 1 cup

Ingredients

1 (8 oz.) pkg. cream
cheese, softened

2½ oz. sliced ham, chopped
2 green onions, chopped

Directions

In a medium bowl, combine cream cheese, chopped ham and chopped green onions. Cover and chill in the refrigerator overnight before serving. Serve with crackers, pita chips or toasted baguette slices for dipping and spreading.

Dip Tip

To keep your serving bowl neat, mix your cold dip in a large bowl, then transfer it to the smaller serving bowl.

Submarine Sandwich Dip

Makes 3½ cups

Ingredients

½ lb. cooked ham,
   thinly sliced

½ lb. Genoa salami,
   thinly sliced

1 lb. processed American
   cheese, sliced

2 C. mayonnaise

2 tsp. dried oregano

1 onion, chopped

½ head iceberg lettuce,
   shredded

2 tomatoes, diced

Directions

Tear the ham, salami and American cheese into small pieces and place pieces in a large bowl. In a medium bowl, blend the mayonnaise and dried oregano. Stir the mayonnaise mixture into the meat and cheese pieces ½ cup at a time. Mix until the meat and cheese pieces are well coated. Add the chopped onion and stir until well blended. Before serving, mix in the lettuce and tomatoes. Serve with hoagie roll pieces or toasted baguette slices for dipping and spreading.

Garlic Blue Cheese Dip

Makes 3 cups

Ingredients

1 (8 oz.) pkg. cream cheese,
  room temperature
3 oz. blue cheese, crumbled
3 cloves garlic, minced

¼ C. minced onion
4 tsp. Worcestershire sauce
⅛ tsp. hot pepper sauce
1 tsp. salt

Directions

In a medium bowl, beat the cream cheese with an electric mixer until light and creamy. Blend in the crumbled blue cheese, minced garlic, minced onion, Worcestershire sauce, hot pepper sauce and salt. Transfer mixture to serving bowl, cover and chill in the refrigerator until serving. Serve with crackers, apple slices or pita chips for dipping and spreading.

Fruit Infused Guacamole

Makes 1½ cups

Ingredients

2 avocados, peeled, pitted
   and mashed

1½ tsp. lime juice

1½ tsp. orange juice

1½ tsp. pineapple juice

¼ tsp. ground cumin

¼ C. chopped cilantro

Salt to taste

1 tsp. hot pepper sauce,
   optional

Directions

In a large bowl, combine the mashed avocados, lime juice, orange juice, pineapple juice, ground cumin, chopped cilantro and salt; mix well. Add hot pepper sauce if desired. Serve immediately with tortilla chips, lime flavored tortilla chips, carrot sticks and celery sticks.

Dip Tip

Similar to apples, when exposed to air, the surface of guacamole will begin to brown due to oxidation. If you are not serving guacamole immediately, be sure to cover it tightly and store in the refrigerator to slow the color change. Mix thoroughly before serving.

Awesomely Easy Guacamole

Makes 2 cups

Ingredients

2 avocados, peeled, pitted
   and mashed

½ lemon, juiced

2 T. chopped onion

½ tsp. salt

2 T. olive oil

Directions

In a medium bowl, combine the mashed avocados, lemon juice, chopped onion, salt and olive oil. Cover tightly and chill in the refrigerator for 1 hour before serving. Serve with tortilla chips, lime flavored tortilla chips, carrot sticks, celery sticks or red, yellow and green bell pepper strips for dipping.

Dip Tip

Don't be afraid to color coordinate! If you have a colorful dip, try choosing dippers that match to enhance the colors of the ingredients. Serving your dip in a colorful bowl will also dress up your display. Brightly colored serving pieces and dippers will breathe new life into a rather bland looking dip that actually tastes great!

Creamy Cranberry Horseradish Spread

Makes 3 cups

Ingredients

1 (16 oz.) can cranberry sauce
½ C. sugar
⅓ C. minced onion
2 T. horseradish

Salt to taste
1 (8 oz.) pkg. cream cheese, in block form

Directions

In a medium saucepan, combine cranberry sauce, sugar, minced onion and horseradish; bring to a boil. Reduce heat and let simmer for 2 to 3 minutes. Remove from heat and transfer to a medium bowl. Cover and chill in the refrigerator until serving. To serve, place the block of softened cream cheese on a serving plate and pour cranberry mixture over top. Serve with crackers and toasted baguette slices for dipping and spreading.

Parmesan Caesar Dip

Makes 2 cups

Ingredients

1 (8 oz.) pkg. cream
  cheese, softened
1 C. grated Parmesan cheese
½ C. Caesar salad dressing

1 C. chopped romaine lettuce
½ C. croutons

Directions

In a medium bowl, beat cream cheese, grated Parmesan cheese and Caesar dressing on medium speed with an electric mixer. Spread the mixture on the bottom of a 9″ pie plate. Sprinkle chopped romaine lettuce and croutons over the cheese mixture. Sprinkle additional Parmesan cheese over the top if desired. Serve with crackers, an assortment of breaded vegetables, chunked mini bagels, toasted baguette slices and pita chips for dipping.

Pesto Cream Cheese Spread

Makes 2⅓ cups

Ingredients

1 (8 oz.) pkg. cream
  cheese, softened

3 T. milk

⅓ C. pesto sauce

1 red bell pepper,
  finely chopped

Directions

In a medium bowl, blend cream cheese and milk until smooth with an electric mixer on medium speed. Add pesto sauce and chopped red pepper; blend until well combined. Chill in the refrigerator until serving. Serve with hard or soft breadsticks, pita chips, pretzels, crackers, carrot sticks, celery sticks or red, yellow and green bell pepper strips for dipping.

Dip Tip

To discourage guests from double dipping, place a portion of the dip in several individual shot glasses instead of serving in one large bowl. This way each guest may have their own personal serving.

Basic Baba Ghanoush

Makes 1 ½ cups

Ingredients

1 eggplant
¼ C. lemon juice
¼ C. tahini
2 T. sesame seeds

2 cloves garlic, minced
Salt and pepper to taste
1½ T. olive oil

Directions

Preheat the oven to 400°. Using a fork, prick holes in the skin of the eggplant and place on a lightly greased baking sheet. Roast eggplant in the oven for 30 to 40 minutes, turning occasionally, until soft. Remove eggplant from oven and place in a large bowl of cold water; when cool, peel off skin. Place eggplant, lemon juice, tahini, sesame seeds and minced garlic into a blender and puree until smooth. Season with salt and pepper and transfer mixture to a medium bowl; slowly stir in olive oil. Chill in the refrigerator for 3 hours before serving. Serve with pita chips, crackers, carrot sticks, celery sticks or red, yellow and green bell pepper strips for dipping.

Dip Tip

Baba Ghanoush or "eggplant salad" is a popular Middle Eastern dish made primarily of eggplant mashed and mixed with various herbs and seasonings. The eggplant is usually baked or broiled before peeling so that the pulp is soft and has a smoky taste.

Brewer's Cheese Spread

Makes 4 cups

Ingredients

2 (8 oz.) pkgs. cream
  cheese, softened
2 (8 oz.) pkgs. shredded
  Cheddar cheese

½ tsp. garlic powder
½ C. beer

Directions

In a large bowl, combine cream cheese, shredded Cheddar cheese, garlic powder and beer. Using an electric mixer, blend on medium speed until smooth. Transfer mixture to a serving bowl, cover and chill in the refrigerator 30 minutes before serving. Serve with pita chips, crackers, carrot sticks, pretzels or red and green bell pepper strips for dipping.

Dip Tip

Try serving this tasty dip in a hollowed-out head of lettuce, green or red bell pepper. It will add a little color, pizzazz and even some flavor!

Vidalia Provolone Dip

Makes 5 cups

Ingredients

2 C. chopped Vidalia onion   2 C. shredded provolone cheese
1 C. mayonnaise

Directions

Preheat the oven to 350°. In a medium bowl, mix together the chopped Vidalia onion, mayonnaise and provolone cheese. Transfer mixture to an 8″ baking dish. Bake in the oven for 30 minutes or until the onions are tender and top is golden. Serve with onion rings, butter crackers, wheat crackers or pita chips for dipping.

Dip Tip

Dress up your dip by garnishing it with a dollop of sour cream or yogurt. Or, sprinkle paprika or fresh herbs over the dip.

Cream Cheese Chili Dip

Makes 3 cups

Ingredients

1 (8 oz.) pkg. cream
  cheese, softened

1 (15 oz.) can chili with beans

Pinch of chili powder

1½ tsp. sugar

Directions

Spread the cream cheese over the bottom of a 1½-quart microwave-safe baking dish. Spread the chili with beans over the cream cheese. Cover baking dish and microwave on full power for 5 minutes or until the chili and cream cheese become hot and bubbly. Remove dish from microwave and sprinkle chili powder and sugar over the chili with beans. Serve dip hot with tortilla chips or potato skins for dipping and spreading.

Slow-Cooked Italian Sausage Dip

Makes 6½ cups

Ingredients

1 lb. ground Italian sausage

2 tomatoes, chopped

2 green bell peppers, chopped

2 onions, chopped

2 (4 oz.) cans chopped green
  chiles, drained

1 (16 oz.) container
  sour cream

1 (8 oz.) pkg. cream
  cheese, softened

Directions

Place ground Italian sausage in a large deep skillet and cook over medium-high heat until evenly browned. Drain the grease from the skillet and set meat aside. In a large bowl, mix together cooked sausage, chopped tomatoes, chopped green bell peppers, chopped onions, green chiles, sour cream and cream cheese. Transfer dip mixture to a slow cooker. Cook for 1 hour on high heat or until vegetables are soft. Reduce heat and simmer until ready to serve. Serve dip hot with tortilla chips, soft warm breadsticks, toasted garlic bread or breaded mozzarella sticks for dipping.

Mozzarella Artichoke Dip

Makes 5 cups

Ingredients

2 (6.5 oz.) jars marinated
artichoke hearts, drained
and chopped

2 C. shredded mozzarella
cheese

1 C. grated Parmesan cheese

1 C. mayonnaise

½ C. sliced almonds, optional

Directions

Preheat the oven to 275°. In a shallow baking dish, combine the chopped artichoke hearts, shredded mozzarella cheese, grated Parmesan cheese and mayonnaise. Bake in the oven for 45 minutes or until hot and bubbly. Remove from oven and sprinkle sliced almonds over dip if desired. Serve artichoke dip hot with tortilla chips, pita chips or crackers for dipping.

Butternut Squash Dip

Makes 2½ cups

Ingredients

1 medium butternut squash,
   halved and seeded

3 T. olive oil

1 whole head garlic

1 (11 oz.) log goat cheese

1 lemon, juiced

¼ C. finely chopped walnuts

Directions

Preheat the oven to 350°. Brush the cut side of the squash halves with some of the olive oil; place squash oiled side down on a baking sheet. Cut off the top of the garlic head. Drizzle the remaining olive oil over the head of garlic. Wrap garlic in aluminum foil and place on the baking sheet next to squash. Bake in the oven 40 minutes or until the squash can be easily pierced with a fork. Remove from oven and scoop the squash out of the skin; transfer to a medium serving bowl. Squeeze the cloves of garlic out of their skins into the bowl with the squash. Mash garlic and squash until smooth. Break the goat cheese into pieces. Stir goat cheese and lemon juice into squash mixture until well blended. Sprinkle chopped walnuts over the top before serving. Serve dip warm or at room temperature with tortilla chips, pita chips or toasted baguette slices for dipping.

Slow-Cooked Cheesy Chicken Dip

Makes 5 to 6 cups

Ingredients

2 (10 oz.) cans chunk chicken

4 (8 oz.) pkgs. cream cheese, softened

1 (10.75 oz.) can cream of chicken soup

1 (20 oz.) can cream of chicken soup

Chopped jalapeno peppers, to taste

Directions

Combine chunk chicken, cream cheese, both cans cream of chicken soup and chopped jalapenos in a slow cooker; mix well. Cook on low for 1 to 2 hours until heated through. Serve dip warm with tortilla chips, pieces of sourdough bread or crackers for dipping.

Dip Tip

This recipe would look and taste great served in a warm bread bowl. For an easy bread bowl, purchase a 1-pound loaf of frozen bread dough. Let the bread dough thaw in the refrigerator overnight. Once thawed, cut the dough in half and shape each section into a round dome. Place halves on a baking sheet, cover and let the dough rise for 4 to 7 hours depending on the temperature of your kitchen. Preheat the oven to 350°. Bake bread dough in the oven for 20 to 25 minutes or until golden brown. Remove from oven and let cool. Cut the top ¼ off the round loaf of bread and set aside. Remove the insides of the loaf and save bread pieces for dipping. To serve, spoon hot dip into the loaf and replace the top of the loaf.

Cheesy Baked Jalapeno Dip

Makes 4½ cups

Ingredients

2 C. shredded Cheddar cheese

1 C. mayonnaise

1 (2.75 oz.) can chopped black olives, drained, divided

1 (4 oz.) can diced jalapeno peppers, drained

¼ tsp. garlic powder

Dash of hot pepper sauce

1 tomato, chopped

½ C. chopped green onions

Directions

Preheat the oven to 350°. In a large mixing bowl, combine the shredded Cheddar cheese, mayonnaise, half of the chopped black olives, diced jalapeno peppers, garlic and hot pepper sauce. Spread the mixture in the bottom of a 9″ pie pan. Bake in the oven for 20 minutes or until heated through. Remove pie pan from oven and sprinkle the remaining chopped black olives, chopped tomato and chopped green onions over the dip. Serve dip warm with tortilla chips for dipping.

Baked Mozzarella Dip

Makes 5 cups

Ingredients

4 C. shredded mozzarella
   cheese

1 C. mayonnaise

3 cloves garlic, minced

1 (2.25 oz.) can sliced black
   olives, drained

2 fresh jalapeno peppers,
   diced, divided

1 tsp. garlic salt

Directions

Preheat the oven to 350°. In a medium bowl, mix the shredded mozzarella cheese, mayonnaise, minced garlic, sliced black olives and 1 diced jalapeno pepper. Spread the mixture into the bottom of an 8″ baking dish. Season mixture with garlic salt and sprinkle remaining diced jalapeno pepper over top. Bake in the oven for 20 minutes or until the edges are golden brown. Serve with tortilla chips or corn chips for dipping.

White Bean Dip

Makes 1 cup

Ingredients

2 garlic cloves, peeled
2 tsp. minced fresh rosemary
2½ T. olive oil, divided

1 (16 oz.) can white
beans, undrained

Directions

In a medium skillet over medium heat, sauté garlic cloves and minced fresh rosemary in 2 tablespoons of olive oil until ingredients begin to simmer. Add white beans and liquid to the skillet. Mash beans and garlic while cooking in the skillet until mixture is of spreadable consistency. Transfer bean dip to a medium bowl and drizzle with remaining olive oil. To serve, spread bean dip over crusty or toasted bread, topped with a slice of Havarti cheese.

Dip Tip

White beans are also known as Great Northern beans. Similar to the smaller navy bean, Great Northern beans are related to kidney beans and pinto beans. Most white beans eaten in the United States are grown in the Midwest.

Creamy Pepperoni Dip

Makes 4½ cups

Ingredients

1 (8 oz.) pkg. cream
  cheese, softened
½ C. sour cream
⅛ tsp. garlic powder
¼ tsp. dried oregano
1 C. pizza sauce

½ C. sliced pepperoni
¼ C. chopped onion
¼ C. chopped green bell pepper
1 C. shredded mozzarella
  cheese

Directions

Preheat the oven to 350°. In a small bowl, combine cream cheese, sour cream, garlic powder and dried oregano. Spread the mixture into the bottom of a 9″ glass pie pan. Spread pizza sauce over the cream cheese mixture. Arrange the pepperoni slices, chopped onion and chopped green bell pepper over the pizza sauce. Bake in the oven for 10 minutes. Remove from oven and sprinkle shredded mozzarella cheese over top the pie pan. Return to the oven and bake until the cheese has melted. Serve with garlic bread, breaded mozzarella sticks or soft warm breadsticks for dipping.

Slow-Cooked
Double Bean Dip

Makes 5 cups

Ingredients

2 (16 oz.) cans refried beans

1 (15 oz.) can black beans,
   drained and rinsed

1 (15 oz.) can whole kernel
   corn, drained

2 large tomatoes, chopped

Directions

Combine refried beans, black beans, whole kernel corn and chopped tomatoes in a slow-cooker and heat on low, stirring often. Serve bean dip with tortilla chips or melba toast for dipping and spreading.

Dip Tip

This bean dip also tastes delicious as a filler for tacos or burritos.

Red Hot Chicken Dip

Makes 5 cups

Ingredients

*2 (10 oz.) cans chunk
chicken, drained*

¾ C. hot pepper sauce

*2 (8 oz.) pkgs. cream
cheese, softened*

1 C. ranch-style salad dressing

*1½ C. shredded Cheddar
cheese, divided*

Directions

In a medium skillet over medium heat, cook chunk chicken and hot pepper sauce until heated through. Stir in cream cheese and ranch dressing. Cook and stir until well blended and warm. Mix in half of the shredded Cheddar cheese and transfer the mixture to a slow cooker. Sprinkle the remaining shredded Cheddar cheese over the top; cover and cook on low setting until hot and bubbly. Serve with celery sticks and chicken-flavored crackers for dipping.

Dip Tip

This recipe would look and taste great served in a warm bread bowl. See page 55 for an easy bread bowl recipe using frozen dough.

Beefy Baked Taco Dip

Makes 5 to 6 cups

Ingredients

1½ lbs. ground beef

1½ C. shredded Cheddar
   cheese, divided

¾ C. taco sauce

2 (4 oz.) cans green
   chiles, drained

Chopped jalapeno, to taste

2 (16 oz.) cans refried beans

½ C. guacamole dip

½ C. sour cream

1 medium tomato, chopped

½ C. sliced black olives

Directions

Preheat the oven to 400°. In a large skillet over medium high heat, cook and crumble ground beef until browned. Drain grease from skillet. Spread ground beef across the bottom of a 9 x 13″ baking dish. Sprinkle 1 cup shredded Cheddar cheese over the ground beef. Pour taco sauce over the cheese and sprinkle green chiles over the taco sauce. Place chopped jalapenos over the green chiles and spread refried beans on top of the jalapenos. Bake in the oven for 20 minutes or until heated through. Remove from oven and layer with guacamole, sour cream, chopped tomato, sliced black olives and remaining shredded Cheddar cheese. Serve warm with tortilla chips for dipping.

Parmesan Crab Dip

Makes 4 cups

Ingredients

2 (8 oz.) pkgs. cream
  cheese, softened

2 (6 oz.) cans crabmeat,
  drained and flaked

½ C. shredded
  Parmesan cheese

¼ C. chopped green onions

2 tsp. horseradish sauce

Directions

Preheat the oven to 350°. In a large bowl, combine cream cheese, crabmeat, shredded Parmesan cheese, chopped green onions and horseradish sauce. Using an electric mixer on medium speed, blend well. Spoon mixture into a 9″ pie plate. Bake in the oven for 25 to 30 minutes or until lightly browned. Serve warm with crackers or toasted baguette slices for dipping.

Dip Tip

Avoid letting dips with mayonnaise, raw eggs, seafood or meat sit at room temperature for more than two hours.

Warm Neufchâtel
and Salsa Verde

Makes 2 cups

Ingredients

1 (8 oz.) pkg. Neufchâtel cheese   ½ C. chopped fresh cilantro
1 C. mild green salsa
  (salsa verde)

Directions

Cut Neufchâtel into 10 equal pieces and place in a microwave-safe bowl. Cook, uncovered, in the microwave for 1 minute on high heat. Remove from microwave and pour salsa over the cheese and sprinkle with chopped cilantro. Serve warm with tortilla chips, breadsticks, carrot sticks, celery sticks and red pepper strips for dipping.

Dip Tip

Not sure how much dip to make? Since it's hard to tell how hungry your guests will be, a general estimate of ¼ cup of dip per person is a good place to start.

Seven-Layer Fiesta Dip

Makes 5½ cups

Ingredients

1 (15 oz.) can pinto beans, drained and rinsed

1 C. mild to medium salsa, divided

2 green onions, finely chopped, divided

1 small clove garlic, minced

1 C. shredded Monterey Jack cheese

1 (2.75 oz.) can sliced black olives, drained and rinsed

2 medium ripe avocados

⅓ C. chopped fresh cilantro, divided

3 T. minced red onion

2 T. lime juice

½ tsp. salt

1 C. sour cream

Directions

Preheat the oven to 350°. In a medium bowl, combine pinto beans, 3 tablespoons of salsa, half the green onions and minced garlic. Mash ingredients until well combined but still a little chunky. Spread into the bottom of a 9″ glass pie plate. Sprinkle shredded Monterey Jack cheese over the bean mixture and spread remaining salsa over the cheese. Sprinkle sliced black olives over the salsa. Bake in the oven for 15 minutes or until heated through. Cut each avocado in half and remove the pit. Using a spoon, scoop out the fleshy part of the avocado and place in a medium bowl. Using a fork, mash avocado until chunky. Mix in ¼ cup cilantro, minced red onion, lime juice and salt. Remove the hot dip from the oven and spoon the avocado mixture over it. Spread sour cream over the avocado mixture and sprinkle with remaining green onions and cilantro. Serve dip with tortilla chips, taquitos or quesadillas for dipping.

Dip Tip

The two most common varieties of avocados are the rough-skinned, almost black Hass and the smooth, thin-skinned green Fuerte. Although they are similar in size, the Hass has a smaller pit and a more buttery texture than the Fuerte avocado.

Dreamy Orange Dip

Makes 2 cups

Ingredients

1 (7 oz.) jar marshmallow cream

1 (8 oz.) pkg. cream cheese, softened

2 T. frozen orange juice concentrate, thawed

Directions

In a medium bowl, mix together marshmallow cream, cream cheese and orange juice concentrate. Chill in the refrigerator until serving. Serve with fresh orange slices, apples slices, grapes, melon pieces, strawberries or pretzels for dipping.

Dip Tip

Instead of serving sweet fruit dips in a bowl, transfer them to a hollowed out melon, grapefruit or coconut. The "fruit bowl" will not only add a little creativity to your table, but might even add a little extra flavor to your dip.

Strawberry Piña Colada Dip

Makes 1¾ cups

Ingredients

1 (8 oz.) pkg. cream
  cheese, softened

2 T. sugar

6 T. piña colada mix

2 T. light rum

2 T. frozen strawberry
  daiquiri mix, optional

Directions

In a medium bowl, whip together cream cheese, sugar, piña colada mix, light rum and strawberry daiquiri mix. Transfer to a serving bowl and chill in the refrigerator at least 3 hours before serving. Serve with strawberries, banana rounds, melon pieces, pineapple chunks, apple slices or coconut shrimp for dipping.

Dip Tip

Instead of serving this tropical dip in a bowl, try displaying and serving it in a margarita or daiquiri glass. Place the glass in the center of a serving plate or platter and arrange the dippers around it on the plate.

Caramel Chocolate Dip

Makes 1 ½ cups

Ingredients

1 (8 oz.) pkg. caramel candies
2 (1 oz.) squares semi-sweet
  chocolate

½ C. milk

Directions

In a small saucepan over medium heat, melt unwrapped caramels, semi-sweet chocolate and milk, stirring until smooth. Let cool before transferring to a serving bowl. Chill in the refrigerator for 45 minutes to 1 hour. Serve with granola chunks, apple slices, pear slices, banana rounds, dried apricots, marshmallows, walnuts, vanilla wafers or graham cracker sticks for dipping.

Cinnamon Peanut Butter Dip

Makes 2 cups

Ingredients

1 C. vanilla yogurt

½ C. peanut butter

⅛ tsp. ground cinnamon

½ C. whipped topping

Directions

In a medium bowl, combine the vanilla yogurt, peanut butter and ground cinnamon; mix well. Fold in the whipped topping. Chill in the refrigerator until ready to serve. Serve with apple slices, pear slices, vanilla wafers or graham cracker sticks for dipping.

Dip Tip

If you are serving dip in a pretty serving bowl, set one or two spoons in or next to the bowl to encourage guests to put some on their plate instead of hovering over the food table.

Sweet and Snappy Dip

Makes 3 cups

Ingredients

1 (8 oz.) pkg. cream
cheese, softened

1 C. powdered sugar

2 tsp. pumpkin pie spice

1 (8 oz.) container frozen
whipped topping, thawed

Directions

In a small mixing bowl, combine the cream cheese, powdered sugar and pumpkin pie spice using an electric mixer. Beat in whipped topping until blended. Transfer to a serving bowl and refrigerate until serving. This dip is meant to be served with gingersnap cookies for dipping, but also tastes great with apple slices, pear slices, vanilla wafers or graham cracker sticks.

Pumpkin Pie Fluff

Makes 4 ½ cups

Ingredients

1 (5 oz.) pkg. instant vanilla
  pudding mix
1 (15 oz.) can solid pack
  pumpkin

1 tsp. pumpkin pie spice
1 (16 oz.) container frozen
  whipped topping, thawed

Directions

In a large bowl, combine the instant vanilla pudding mix, solid pack pumpkin and pumpkin pie spice; mix well. Fold in the whipped topping. Chill in the refrigerator until serving. Serve with graham cracker sticks or cinnamon graham crackers for dipping.

Dip Tip

To celebrate the fall season in style,
serve this dip in a hollowed-out gourd or pumpkin.

Sweet Butterscotch Dip

Makes 6 to 7 cups

Ingredients

2 (14 oz.) cans sweetened
  condensed milk

2 (12 oz.) bags butterscotch
  morsels

2 T. unsalted butter

2 T. white vinegar

1 T. ground cinnamon

1 T. vanilla extract

Directions

In a medium saucepan over medium heat, combine sweetened condensed milk, butterscotch morsels, unsalted butter, white vinegar, ground cinnamon and vanilla extract. Cook until melted. Let cool slightly and transfer to a serving bowl. Serve with apple slices, pear slices, melon pieces, banana rounds, vanilla wafers, chocolate graham cracker sticks, strawberries, grapes and bananas for dipping.

Creamy Cup of Joe Dip

Makes 3½ cups

Ingredients

1 (8 oz.) pkg. cream
cheese, softened

1 (8 oz.) container
sour cream

½ C. brown sugar

⅓ C. coffee-flavored liqueur

1 (8 oz.) container frozen
whipped topping, thawed

Directions

In a medium bowl, blend together the cream cheese, sour cream, brown sugar and coffee-flavored liqueur until smooth. Fold in the whipped topping. Transfer to a serving bowl and chill in the refrigerator until serving. Serve dip with apple slices, pear slices, melon pieces, strawberries, grapes, banana rounds or mini biscotti cookies for dipping.

Dip Tip

Instead of serving this coffee-inspired dip in a bowl, try displaying it in a coffee or latte mug. For individual servings, transfer a portion of the dip to espresso cups for each party guest. Arrange fresh fruit pieces on the saucer around the cup. Place a dab of whipped topping on top of the dip and sprinkle with chocolate shavings to garnish.

Slow-Cooked Caramel Dip

Makes 4 ½ cups

Ingredients

1 (14 oz.) pkg. caramel candies

1 (14 oz.) can sweetened
  condensed milk

1 C. shredded coconut

½ C. pecan pieces

Directions

Unwrap caramels and place in a slow-cooker with sweetened condensed milk, shredded coconut and pecan pieces. Cook on low for 90 minutes, stirring after 30 minutes. Stir again after 70 or 80 minutes of cooking. Cook until caramels are completely melted. Transfer caramel dip to a bowl and serve warm with apple slices, pear slices, brownie pieces and pound cake cut into cubes for dipping.

Dip Tip

To keep apple slices from turning brown when serving them with dip, squeeze or spray a small amount of lemon or lime juice over each slice. The acid slows down the oxidation process that browns apples. Be careful not to overdo it; you don't want your apples to taste like lemons!

Chocolate Coconut Cream Cheese Dip

Makes 3 cups

Ingredients

1 (8 oz.) pkg. cream
cheese, softened

1 C. semi-sweet chocolate chips

½ C. flaked coconut, toasted*

½ C. chopped peanuts

Directions

Spread cream cheese into the bottom of a 9″ microwave-safe glass pie plate or quiche dish. Sprinkle chocolate chips over the cream cheese and top with toasted flaked coconut and chopped peanuts. Cook in the microwave on medium power for 3 to 4 minutes or until warmed through. Remove from microwave and serve warm with graham crackers, graham cracker sticks or shortbread cookies for dipping.

To toast, place coconut flakes in a single layer on a baking sheet. Bake at 350° for 8 to 10 minutes or until coconut flakes are golden brown.

Wild Blueberry Salsa

Makes 3 to 4 cups

Ingredients

2 medium tomatoes

1 C. fresh or frozen
  wild blueberries

¾ C. chopped sweet onion

2 cloves garlic, minced

1 jalapeno pepper,
  finely chopped

½ fresh chile, finely chopped

2 T. chopped fresh cilantro

2 T. chopped fresh parsley

2 T. rice vinegar

2 T. olive oil

Salt and pepper to taste

Directions

Bring a lightly salted pot of water to a boil. Score the skin on the bottom of each tomato by slicing an X-shape. Place the tomatoes in the pot and cook for 15 minutes. Remove from pot and place tomatoes in a bowl of cold water. Once cool, carefully peel off the skins, cut in half, remove and discard seeds and chop the tomatoes. In a medium bowl, combine the chopped tomatoes, wild blueberries, chopped onion, minced garlic, chopped jalapeno pepper, chopped chile pepper, chopped cilantro and chopped parsley. Add the rice vinegar and olive oil; stir gently to mix, and season with salt and pepper. Cover salsa and chill in the refrigerator overnight to allow flavors to blend. Depending on how juicy the tomatoes are, salsa may need to be slightly drained before serving. Serve with tortilla chips for dipping.

Simply Salsa

Makes 4 to 5 cups

Ingredients

4 large tomatoes, chopped
1 onion, chopped
½ C. chopped fresh cilantro
3 cloves garlic, minced
1 T. lime juice

1 tomatillo, diced, optional
Salt to taste
1 jalapeno pepper, minced,
   to taste

Directions

In a medium bowl, combine chopped tomatoes, chopped onion, chopped cilantro, minced garlic, lime juice, diced tomatillo and salt; mix well. Add the jalapeno to desired taste. Cover salsa and chill in the refrigerator until ready to serve. Serve with tortilla chips, taquitos or quesadillas for dipping.

Dip Tip

For a quick and easy cheese quesadilla, place a 6″ flour tortilla on a greased baking sheet. Cover it with ¼ cup of salsa and ½ cup of shredded Cheddar cheese. Place another 6″ flour tortilla on top of the cheese. Cook under the broiler, 4″ from heat source, for 3 minutes on each side or until golden brown. Cut into wedges to serve with salsa or Mexican-style dips.

Spicy Blender Salsa

Makes 4 to 5 cups

Ingredients

2 (14.5 oz.) cans diced
   tomatoes

1½ (10 oz.) cans diced
   tomatoes with green
   chiles

2 T. lemon juice

1 fresh jalapeno pepper,
   chopped

⅓ C. chopped fresh cilantro

1 small yellow onion, chopped

3 drops hot pepper sauce

1 clove garlic, minced

Directions

Place diced tomatoes, diced tomatoes with green chiles, lemon juice, chopped jalapeno pepper, chopped cilantro, chopped yellow onion, hot pepper sauce and minced garlic in a blender. Blend until smooth. Chill in the refrigerator until serving. Serve with tortilla chips, taquitos or quesadillas for dipping.

Summer Mango Salsa

Makes 3 to 4 cups

Ingredients

1 mango, peeled, seeded and diced

1 avocado, peeled, pitted and diced

4 tomatoes, diced

1 jalapeno pepper, seeded and minced

½ C. chopped fresh cilantro

3 cloves garlic, minced

1 tsp. salt

2 T. fresh lime juice

¼ C. chopped red onion

3 T. olive oil

Directions

In a medium bowl, combine the diced mango, diced avocado, diced tomatoes, minced jalapeno, chopped cilantro and minced garlic. Stir in the salt, lime juice, chopped red onion and olive oil. Chill in the refrigerator for about 30 minutes to allow flavors to blend. Serve salsa with tortilla chips for dipping.

Dip Tip

This salsa also tastes great served over grilled salmon or chicken.

Broiled Tomato Salsa

Makes 2 to 3 cups

Ingredients

4 large ripe tomatoes,
   halved and seeded

½ red onion, minced

2 cloves garlic, peeled
   and crushed

2 red chiles, seeded
   and minced

½ C. chopped fresh cilantro

1 T. olive oil

1 T. lemon juice

Salt and pepper to taste

Directions

Preheat the broiler. Place tomato halves on a baking sheet. Broil tomatoes for 5 minutes, turning occasionally, until darkened. Remove tomatoes from under broiler and place in a small sealed container; allow tomatoes to cool for 15 to 20 minutes. Once cooled, remove and discard tomato skins. Chop tomatoes and place in a medium bowl. Add minced red onion, minced garlic, red chile peppers, chopped cilantro, olive oil, lemon juice, salt and pepper. Cover and chill in the refrigerator 1 hour before serving. Serve with tortilla chips, taquitos or quesadillas for dipping.

Habanero Fruit Salsa

Makes 3 to 4 cups

Ingredients

5 kiwis, peeled and diced

4 C. chopped strawberries

2 C. chopped fresh blackberries

4 Granny Smith apples,
  peeled, cored and shredded

2 T. fruit jelly, any flavor

¾ C. brown sugar

1 T. cayenne pepper

3 T. habanero hot sauce

1 (7 oz.) can green salsa

⅓ C. lime juice

Directions

In a large bowl, combine the diced kiwis, chopped strawberries, chopped blackberries and shredded apples. Stir in the fruit jelly, brown sugar, cayenne pepper, habanero hot sauce, green salsa and lime juice; mix well. Chill in the refrigerator until serving. Serve with tortilla chips, lime flavored tortilla chips or pita chips for dipping.

Strawberry Salsa

Makes 2½ cups

Ingredients

2 C. chopped strawberries

1 ripe mango, peeled, pitted
and chopped

1 to 2 jalapeno peppers, seeded
and chopped

¼ C. chopped fresh cilantro

Dash of salt

Dash of sugar

2 T. lime juice

Directions

In a medium bowl, mix together chopped strawberries, chopped mango, chopped jalapeno peppers, chopped cilantro, salt, sugar and lime juice. Let stand at least 30 minutes to allow flavors to combine. Serve salsa with tortilla chips for dipping.

Cucumber Lime Salsa

Makes 1 cup

Ingredients

1 lime

*1 cucumber, peeled
and chopped*

¾ C. mild salsa

2 T. chopped fresh cilantro

Directions

Grate 1 teaspoon of peel from the lime and squeeze 2 tablespoons of juice from the lime. In a small bowl, combine lime peel, lime juice, chopped cucumber, mild salsa and chopped cilantro. Cover and chill in the refrigerator for 1 day. Serve with tortilla chips or lime tortilla chips for dipping.

Dip Tip

This salsa also tastes great served over grilled or broiled fish.

Perfect Pita Chips

Makes 8 dozen chips

Ingredients

12 pita bread pockets
½ C. olive oil
½ tsp. pepper

1 tsp. garlic salt
½ tsp. dried basil
1 tsp. dried chervil

Directions

Preheat the oven to 400°. Cut each pita bread into 8 wedges. Place the wedges on a lined baking sheet. In a small bowl, combine the olive oil, pepper, garlic salt, dried basil and dried chervil; mix well. Brush each pita wedge with the oil mixture. Bake in the oven for 7 minutes or until golden and crispy. Keep a close watch on the pita chips while in the oven as they tend to burn easily. Remove from oven and let cool. Serve pita chips as dippers for cold dips, hot dips, hummus and salsa.

Dipper Tip

If you're a cheese lover, try sprinkling a little grated Parmesan cheese over each pita wedge before baking.

Tasty Tortilla Chips

Makes 6 ½ dozen chips

Ingredients

2 T. butter or margarine,
  melted
10 (7") flour tortillas

¾ tsp. garlic salt
¾ tsp. ground cumin
¾ tsp. chili powder

Directions

Preheat the oven to 400°. Brush melted butter or margarine over both sides of each flour tortilla. In a small bowl, combine garlic salt, ground cumin and chili powder; mix well. Sprinkle mixture over both sides of each tortilla. Cut each tortilla into 8 wedges and place on an ungreased baking sheet. Bake in the oven for 6 to 8 minutes or until crisp. Remove from oven and let cool. Serve tortilla chips as dippers with salsa, hummus, hot dips or cold dips.

Dipper Tip

To make a sweet version of these chips, replace the garlic salt mixture with mixture of cinnamon and sugar. Serve these tortilla chips with fruit salsas or sweet dips.

Italian Breadstick Bites

Makes 24 breadsticks

Ingredients

1 (11 oz.) can refrigerated
breadstick dough

¼ C. grated Parmesan cheese

½ tsp. Italian seasoning

Directions

Preheat the oven to 375°. Unroll the breadstick dough and cut in half widthwise; separate the dough into pieces. In a large resealable plastic bag, combine the Parmesan cheese and Italian seasoning; shake to combine. Add breadstick dough pieces to the bag a few at a time and shake to coat. Once coated, place all the breadstick dough pieces on an ungreased baking sheet. Bake in the oven for 10 to 13 minutes or until breadsticks are golden. Remove from oven and let cool slightly. Serve breadsticks warm as dippers for hot dips or tomato-based dips.

Dipper Tip

Don't have the perfect dip to pair with the Italian breadsticks? Place 1 cup of pizza sauce in a microwave-safe bowl and sprinkle ¼ cup of shredded mozzarella cheese over the sauce. Cook in the microwave on high heat for 1 minute or until cheese is melted and bubbly. Serve dipping sauce warm with Italian breadsticks.

Index

Collect all 4 Titles in the
super bowl
Series

the super bowl
50 Sensational Salads

the super bowl
50 Satisfying Soups

the super bowl
50 Pleasing Pastas

from CQ Products